CELEBRATING
FATHER'S DAY

BY ANN HEINRICHS · ILLUSTRATED BY R. W. ALLEY

Published by The Child's World®
1980 Lookout Drive • Mankato, MN 56003-1705
800-599-READ • www.childsworld.com

ISBN 9781503853836 (Reinforced Library Binding)
ISBN 9781503854659 (Portable Document Format)
ISBN 9781503855038 (Online Multi-user eBook)
LCCN: 2021953062

Printed in the United States of America

ABOUT THE AUTHOR

Ann Heinrichs lives in Chicago, Illinois. She has written more than two hundred books for children. She loves traveling to faraway places.

ABOUT THE ILLUSTRATOR

R. W. Alley enjoys drawing pictures of happy families from his home in Rhode Island. He's guided in this effort by his winsome wife and two cheery children.

CONTENTS

CHAPTER 1

Happy Father's Day!

You may call him Daddy, Papa, Father, or Dad. He is strong, wise, and fun. Best of all, he loves you. We have a special holiday just for him. It's Father's Day!

That day, we thank fathers for all they do. We also honor those who are like fathers to us. They may be grandfathers, **stepfathers**, uncles, or big brothers. They might even be neighbors or family friends.

What's the best way to say "Happy Father's Day"? Just say, "I love you!"

I'm just as lucky as I can be
For the world's best
Dad belongs to me!
—Author unknown

Father's Day is a time to say thank you to dads and to all those in our lives who are like dads to us.

5

CHAPTER 2

The First Father's Day Card

A story is told about a boy named Elmesu. He lived almost four thousand years ago. His home was in Mesopotamia (mess-oh-poh-TAY-mee-uh). Part of this **ancient** region is in modern Iraq.

Elmesu made a tablet of wet clay. Using a **reed**, he carefully carved a message on it. He wished his father health. And he wished him a long life.

Elmesu didn't know what he had done. He had made the first Father's Day card!

A wise son makes a glad father.
—The Bible
Proverbs 10:1

Elmesu wrote the first Father's Day card thousands of years ago.

Blessed indeed is the man who hears many gentle voices call him father!
—Lydia M. Child
(1802–1880)

CHAPTER 3

How Did Father's Day Begin?

Who started Father's Day? A loving daughter! Her name was Sonora Smart Dodd.

Sonora grew up on a farm in Washington State in the early 1900s. Her mother died when she was little. Sonora's father, William Smart, was left with six children. He raised them all by himself.

One Mother's Day, Sonora was in church. The **sermon** was about mothers. But Sonora couldn't help thinking about her father. He had been so strong and loving. Suddenly, she had an idea. Why not have a Father's Day?

William Smart raised six children on his own.

In the United States, Father's Day is celebrated on the third Sunday in June.

Father's Day became an official holiday in 1972.

William Smart's birthday was in June. So Sonora suggested a Sunday in June. Her church agreed to hold a service for fathers that day. It was held on June 19, 1910. That was the first Father's Day celebration.

The idea spread quickly. Soon people around the country were celebrating Father's Day. At last, it was made a permanent national holiday in 1972.

BE KIND

Be kind to thy father,
for when thou wert young,
Who loved thee so fondly as he?
He caught the first accents
that fell from thy tongue,
And joined in thy innocent glee.
—Margaret Courtney
(1822-1862)

CHAPTER 4

How Do We Celebrate?

We celebrate Father's Day by showing dads how much we love them! There are many Father's Day **traditions**. One is giving Father's Day cards. Inside the cards are warm and loving messages.

We might have a special dinner just for Dad. Or treat him to his favorite activity. Or give him a gift that has something to do with his hobby. There's one gift he's sure to love. It's a great big hug!

Many people wear a rose on Father's Day. A red rose means the father is living. A white rose means he has died. But a child's love lives forever.

DADDY, I LOVE YOU

Daddy, I love you
For all that you do.
I'll kiss you and hug you
'Cause you love me, too.

You feed me and need me
To teach you to play,
So smile 'cause I love you
On this Father's Day.
—*Author unknown*

Does your dad like fishing? A Father's Day fishing trip might be a good way to celebrate his special day!

FOR DAD!

CHAPTER 5

Fathers of All Kinds

What kinds of fathers are there? All kinds! Just look at George Washington. He's called the Father of Our Country. Other great men helped form the United States. We call them the Founding Fathers.

LITTLE EYES UPON YOU

There are little eyes upon you,
and they're watching night and day.
There are little ears that quickly
take in every word you say.
There are little hands all eager
to do anything you do,
And a little child who's waiting
to grow up to be like you.
—*Author unknown*

George Washington was a father to the new United States.

Albert Einstein fathered many of the important ideas in modern science.

Albert Einstein was a famous scientist. He helped us understand space and time. We have a name for him, too. He's often called the Father of Modern Science.

Some of these men had no children. Yet we look up to them as fathers. They helped us by leading, guiding, and teaching. They were all great fathers to us!

CHAPTER 6

Father's Day around the World

People around the world have a special day for fathers. In many Christian countries, it's March 19. That's Saint Joseph's Day. Joseph was the husband of Mary, Jesus' mother. Joseph lovingly raised Jesus. He became a model for caring fathers.

In Taiwan, Father's Day is August 8. That date—8/8—is pronounced BA BA in Chinese. And *baba* is Chinese for "father!"

Father's Day is a winter holiday in Sweden. It's the second Sunday in November. Fathers get a special cake that day. Children make drawings for their fathers. Some even serve their father breakfast in bed!

My heart is happy, my mind is free. I had a father who talked with me.
—*Hilda Bigelow*

Father's Day is celebrated on August 8 in Taiwan.

Safe, for a child, is his father's hand, holding him tight.
—Marion C. Garretty

CHAPTER 7

Poetry Corner

DADDY'S FOOTSTEPS

"Walk a little slower, Daddy,"
Said a little child so small.
"I'm following in your footsteps,
And I don't want to fall.

"Sometimes your steps are very fast,
Sometimes they're hard to see;
So walk a little slower, Daddy,
For you are leading me.

"Someday when I'm all grown up,
You're what I want to be;
Then I will have a little child
Who'll want to follow me.

"And I would want to lead just right,
And know that I was true;
So walk a little slower, Daddy,
For I must follow you!"

—*Author unknown*

WHAT IS A DAD?

A dad is a person who's loving and kind,
And often he knows what you have on your mind.

He's someone who listens, suggests, and defends—
A dad can be one of your very best friends!

He's proud of your triumphs, but when things go wrong,
A dad can be patient and helpful and strong.

In all that you do, a dad's love plays a part—
There's always a place for him deep in your heart.

And each year that passes, you're even more glad,
More grateful and proud just to call him your dad!

—*Author unknown*

OUR FATHERS

Our fathers toil with hands and heart
To make our lives complete.
They quietly brave the winter cold,
Endure the summer heat.

Our fathers' lives are busy, but
There's always time for us.
They boldly face the ups and downs
And seldom ever fuss.

Our fathers are the greatest dads.
We know you know this, too.
But thank you for the chance to share
Our love for them with you.

—*Author unknown*

CHAPTER 8

Our Grandfathers and Uncles

WALKING WITH GRANDPA

I like to walk with Grandpa,
His steps are short like mine.
He doesn't say, "Now hurry up!"
He always takes his time.

I like to walk with Grandpa,
His eyes see things like mine do—
Wee pebbles bright, a funny cloud,
Half hidden drops of dew.

Children's children are the crown of old men.
—*The Bible, Proverbs 17:6*

Most people have to hurry,
They do not stop and see.
I'm glad that God made Grandpa
Unrushed and young like me.

—*Author unknown*

**Grown men can
learn from very little
children, for the hearts of
little children are pure.**
—*Nicholas Black Elk
(1863–1950)*

MY UNCLE

My uncle's very special—
He's warm and kind, you see.
No matter when I need to talk,
He has time for me.

He teaches me what's right and wrong
And shows me how to be.
He treasures having me around
Just because I'm me.

Thank you, Uncle _____,
For the loving things you do.
I hope that I'll grow up to be
As wonderful as you!

—*Author unknown*

You can tell your uncle
stuff that you could
not tell your dad.
—*Dusty Baker*

SHOWING OUR LOVE ON FATHER'S DAY

* What's your father's favorite meal? Burgers or a steak? Why not have another adult help you cook it for him?

* Do you have a special grandfather, stepfather, or uncle? Show your love by giving him a nice card.

* Do you know someone from another country? Ask if he or she celebrates a special holiday for fathers. Ask what the holiday customs are.

* Is there a home for older people in your community? See if you can visit on Father's Day. Bring cards or flowers for the men. Ask them to tell you about their lives.

MAKING A PORTRAIT FROM VEGETABLES, CHEESE, AND CRACKERS

What you need:
2 cherry tomatoes
1 orange
1 ounce cheddar cheese
8 thin wheat crackers
   (square or rectangular crackers work best)
1/2 cup shredded carrots

Directions

1. Slice the cherry tomatoes in half, and peel and divide the orange.

2. Cut the cheese into a variety of shapes, including squares, triangles, and circles.*

3. Arrange the crackers on a plate so they form a rectangle or square.

4. Use the cheese, tomatoes, orange, and carrots to design your dad's face on the crackers. Two tomato halves can be his eyes, and the shredded carrot is good for hair. Turn an orange slice right side up or upside down to make a smile or frown.

5. Pick a cheese shape that looks most like your dad's nose. Mix and match the ingredients to form different features.

6. Get creative—you could make a face for every member of your family!

*Have an adult (especially a dad) help you with the cutting.

MAKING A PHOTO HOUSE

What you need:

1 sheet of white construction paper
    or other heavyweight paper
1 photo of each member of your family
1 piece of cardboard about the same
    size as your sheet of paper

Scissors
Crayons
Markers
Tape
Glue

Directions

1. Use crayons or markers to draw your house on the sheet of white paper.
2. Draw a window for each member of your family.
3. Cut out the window openings with the scissors. Ask an adult to help with this step.
4. Place a photo behind each window and tape it in place along the edges.
5. Use the scissors to cut out the outline of the house.
6. Place the cutout house face down on the table.
7. Spread glue along the outside edges of the house and place the cardboard on top of the house.
8. Let the glue dry.
9. Ask an adult to help you trim the cardboard so it is the same size as the house.

Now you're ready to present your dad with a special gift. Happy Father's Day!

GLOSSARY

ancient (AYN-shunt)—very old; often meaning thousands of years old

national (NASH-uh-null)—relating to a country

reed (REED)—the stiff stem of a tall grass that grows along the edge of lakes

sermon (SUR-mun)—a speech given in church that teaches a lesson

stepfathers (STEP-fah-thurz)—men who become fathers after marrying women who already have children

traditions (truh-DISH-unz)—long-held customs or something people do every year

LEARN MORE

BOOKS

Bennett, Kelly. *Dad and Pop: An Ode to Fathers and Stepfathers*. Somerville, MA: Candlewick Press, 2010.

Kartes, Danielle. *Grandpa and Me Learn to Cook Together*. Naperville, IL: Sourcebooks Explore, 2020.

Reagan, Jean. *How to Surprise a Dad*. New York, NY: Dragonfly, 2021.

Suen, Anastasia. *Father's Day Gifts*. Vero Beach, FL: Rourke Educational Media, 2018.

Wing. Natasha. *The Night Before Father's Day*. London: Grosset & Dunlap, 2012.

WEBSITES

Visit our website for links about Father's Day and other holidays:
childsworld.com/links

Note to Parents, Teachers, and Librarians: We routinely verify our Web links to make sure they are safe and active sites. So encourage your readers to check them out!

INDEX